Inspired by A. A. Milne

Pooh's Little Book of
Feng Shui

With illustrations by Ernest H. Shepard

Dutton Books 蜜蜂 New York

Copyright © 2000 by Michael John Brown, Peter Janson-Smith, Roger Hugh Vaughan Charles Morgan, and Timothy Michael Robinson, Trustees of the Pooh Properties

Individual copyrights for text and illustrations:
Winnie-the-Pooh, copyright © 1926 by E. P. Dutton & Co., Inc.; copyright renewal 1954 by A. A. Milne. *The House At Pooh Corner,* copyright © 1928 by E. P. Dutton & Co., Inc.; copyright renewal 1956 by A. A. Milne.

CIP Data is available.
Published in the United States by Dutton Children's Books,
a division of Penguin Putnam Books for Young Readers
345 Hudson Street, New York, New York 10014
www.penguinputnam.com

Written by Anna Ludlow
Designed by Richard Amari
Printed in China
First American Edition
1 3 5 7 9 10 8 6 4 2
ISBN 0-525-46331-3

How It All Began

When I told Pooh that I was writing a book about feng shui, Pooh said, "Oh" and "Are you?" and, after a long, thoughtful pause, "Fung what?"

"Feng shui," I said. "It's the ancient Chinese system of living life in harmony with your environment and with the natural rhythms of nature, and of making use of the dynamic flow of energy in the universe, to bring you greater happiness and good fortune."

"Oh," said Pooh, and he thought how wonderful it would be to have a Real Brain that told you things about ancient rhythms and Chinese fortunes. And then he asked carelessly, "Will I be in it anywhere?"

And when I said, "Yes," because living in harmony with nature is what Bears do best, Pooh said to himself, "A book about me. How grand!"

Then Piglet, who had been listening all along, asked whether he would be in the book, too.

"Yes, of course," I said, because bringing happiness to others is what Piglets do best.

But now, before all the others start asking whether they are in it, too, I think perhaps we'd better begin.

What Bears Do Best

The ancient Chinese system of feng shui
can appear complicated at first.

Even a bit abstract.

Chinese symbols are not always easy to interpret.

Especially for a Bear of Very Little Brain.

Feng shui is about creating balance by
living in harmony with nature.

The principles are really very simple to apply,
almost as instinctive as humming a new hum.

Not that Pooh really knows this, because Pooh is a Bear of Very Little Brain, and long words bother him. In fact, *nobody* in the Forest really seems to know what feng shui *is*. They don't know where it came from or when it arrived. Everybody just knows that one day it was there.

When Feng Shui Came to the Hundred Acre Wood

It was Rabbit who came across it first. One day, he saw the words *feng shui* written on a Notice, and he decided that it must have something to do with what Christopher Robin did on Tuesdays. Rabbit thought that if only he could find Christopher Robin, perhaps he could discover who or what feng shui was.

But since it *was* Tuesday, and Christopher Robin had already gone out, Rabbit went to ask Owl instead.

Owl, being Clever, told Rabbit that *feng shui* is pronounced "foong shway." Then he looked Very Wise Indeed when he told Rabbit that it meant "wind and water," but he couldn't explain exactly what it was all about, because Rabbit was looking over his shoulder in an impatient kind of way and making him nervous. But he told Rabbit that he thought feng shui could be found in the Forest. "Ah," said Rabbit, and off he went to ask Pooh if he'd seen it.

"Pooh," asked Rabbit, "have you seen a
feng shui in the Forest at all?"
"No," said Pooh, "not a—no," said Pooh.
"I saw Tigger just now."
"That's no good," said Rabbit.

"A feng shui?" thought Pooh. And then he began
to wonder if a hum about it might come to him,
with words that rhymed with "shway."

"Piglet, have you seen a feng shui
in the Forest?" Rabbit asked Piglet.
"N-no," said Piglet.
"Isn't that one of the Fiercer Animals?"
"That's what I'm trying to find out, Piglet,"
said Rabbit importantly.

"They haven't got any Brains, any of them,"
thought Eeyore, sighing to himself.
"Isn't anyone going to ask me?" he said
to anyone who was listening.
"Always the last to be asked," he added bitterly.

But perhaps, dear reader, while Rabbit is busy looking
for feng shui, I should tell you some of the things about
it that have been found in the Forest, such as how chi flows
and how to balance yin and yang, how to choose a
good place to build your home and how to be
in harmony with nature....

The Flow of Chi

Chi is the flow of energy. Chi can flow up…

. . . or down.

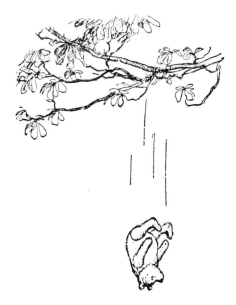

Chi can be auspicious...

...or inauspicious.

A bed facing the east encourages the best flow
of chi to ensure a restful sleep.

Mirrors facing the bed upset the flow of chi, disturbing one's sleep, and can make you, and any guest who might be staying, feel restless in the night.

Feng shui is about harnessing the forces
of energy in nature to be of beneficial effect
to you and your environment.

Sheng chi is good chi. It is created by energy that flows in a meandering fashion. Gently meandering water creates good chi and is especially helpful for playing Poohsticks.

Fast-flowing water is not auspicious.

Too much of it can result in the Need for Rescue.

Shar chi is bad chi. Sharp, spiky things,
like gorse-bushes, create shar chi and are best avoided.

"Do you think honey can make sheng chi?"
said Pooh to Eeyore.
"Honey flows gently," said Pooh thoughtfully.
"And I think I have something Very Important to do,"
he added, going home to do it.

"And I suppose sharp, spiky thistles make shar chi," said Eeyore gloomily, waving a hoof at a patch he had saved.
"Bah!" he said, and he stumped off.

It isn't so funny that a bear likes honey.
Buzz! Buzz! Buzz! Now we know why he does!

Balancing Yin and Yang

Yin and yang are opposites. Yang is active.

Yin is passive.

A good balance of yin and yang is essential.
Too much yang energy can cause accidents…

and confusion…

even nightmares.

Too much noise creates an excess of yang
and can upset the neighbors.

Worraworraworraworraworra.

"What did you say it was?" asked Eeyore.

"Tigger."

"Ah!" said Eeyore.

"He's just come," explained Piglet.

"Ah!" said Eeyore again.

He thought for a long time and then said:

"When is he going?"

Yang is hot.
Yin is cold.
Too much yin energy can lead to…

physical inactivity…

an accumulation of coldness...

and a gloomy state of mind.

Water is one of the best cures
for too much yang energy.
Its calming influence can help create
a better balance of yin and yang.

But those who are by nature very yin
develop a lifelong antipathy to water.

They simply can't be expected to appreciate the benefits.

Those who are *excessively* yin should try to keep away from water altogether.

Wearing red is a very helpful cure for
too much yin energy.

It's surprising how a red ribbon
can turn your bad mood on its head.

"Let's Build It Here," Said Pooh.

If your home is in a place where the light is gloomy, where the land is damp and boggy, and where the winds are harsh and threatening, it will not be a happy home. Feng shui would advise having your house moved to another part of the Forest altogether.

A well-positioned home will be auspicious and bring happiness to its owner. Trees behind a house give it support for good fortune and happiness, while gently undulating land and open space in front of a house bring good luck.

"We will build it here," said Pooh,
"just by this wood, out of the wind,
because this is where I thought of it."

Some friends can never be
relied on to accept gifts
graciously. But if your
gift is based on the
principles of feng
shui, you may
get a surprisingly
positive response.

"Here it is as good as ever,"
said Eeyore.
"In fact, better
in places."
"Much better,"
said Pooh
and Piglet
together.

If your home is in a green and luscious
part of the Forest, chi can wrap itself
around your house, bringing you good luck.

Places that face the direction of a warm breeze
have excellent feng shui.

But a blustery place is *not* blessed with good feng shui.

If you like visitors, arranging your furniture in a friendly way will create a good flow of chi, making them feel welcome and completely at ease.

If you don't like visitors, uncomfortable surroundings will upset the chi, ensuring that they won't stay for long.

If your visitors don't get the message, fill your house with clutter before their next visit. A cluttered house creates an excess of yang energy and makes the chi flow the wrong way.

Don't take your evasive techniques too far—
if the yang energy is *very* excessive,
your home may not last.

Making a Grand Entrance

A welcoming light outside your front door
will ward off negative chi and encourage friends to visit…

...day and night.

A front door by a sharp incline...

...is very inauspicious.

The size of a door is very important.
Large, spacious doors invite good fortune.

And friendly visitors.

Small doors bring bad luck—
and visitors who won't leave,
even when you've asked them politely.

A doorbell creates a good flow of chi.

Unless it belongs to someone else…

and he is feeling lost without it.

Being In Harmony with Nature

The elements of nature need to be in balance to create good feng shui. If the elements of nature are not in balance, it may attract the wrong sort of bees into the Forest. And as Pooh has discovered, the wrong sort of bees make the wrong sort of honey. And when *that* happens, the feng shui is not good *at all*.

Nature is cyclical.
So are Woozle footprints.

Overhead beams and protrusions are inauspicious.
Being underneath them may cause anxiety
and can even be dangerous to your health.

If you come from a hot climate, you will probably
have an excitable, changeable nature.

If you come from a gray, damp climate, you will probably
have a gray, damp nature—don't try to fight it.

If you come from a hot climate, you may find that those from a gray, damp climate don't always welcome your enthusiasm.

Avoid…

being exposed…

to the elements.

Especially if you already know you don't like them.

If you want to be happy…

...follow your instincts.

Friendlier with Two

If you are looking for friendship, display personal items of sentimental value in pairs in your home.

A single pot of honey is a lonely pot of honey.
It's always friendlier with two.

It Was Here All Along

"Rabbit," said Pooh. "It's been found."
"What has?" said Rabbit.
"Fung...that thing you were
looking for," said Pooh.
"Where is it now?" asked Rabbit.
"Well, I think it's been seen all over
the Forest," said Pooh.
"Then it could be anywhere now," said Rabbit.
"We'd better go and tell Christopher Robin.
Are you coming, Pooh?"

"I don't think so," said Pooh. "It's nearly
eleven o'clock, and I have to go home and do one
or two things. Because I haven't done them yet."
So Pooh went home to do them.

If you want to bring the benefits of feng shui into *your* life and live in harmony with nature, do as Pooh does and find a warm and sunny place to sit in a quiet part of the Forest.

If you spend enough time in that calm and peaceful spot, you will find that much happiness comes your way.

This Warm and Sunny Spot

This warm and sunny Spot
Belongs to Pooh.
And here he wonders what
He's going to do.
Oh, bother, I forgot—
It's Piglet's too.